Autism and Martial Arts:
A Guide for Children, Parents and Teachers

Dr Sandra Beale-Ellis

NAKMAS
PUBLISHING

First Published 2015

NAKMAS Publishing
PO Box 262, Herne Bay, Kent, England, CT6 9AW
Tel. 01227 370055 Fax. 01227 370056
www.nakmaspublishing.com

British Library Cataloguing in Publication Data.
A catalogue record of this book is available from the
British Library.

ISBN 978-0-9933142-0-9

Typesetter / Graphics: Sarah Taffe of Evoke Visual
Photographer: Sam Austin of Sam Austin Design
Printed By: Dolman Scott Ltd

WE LOVE MARTIAL ARTS, WILL YOU?

**" I am blessed to
be different.
Without AUTISM the world
might be quite dreary. "**

Dr Sandra Beale-Ellis

DEDICATION

To my husband Joe who unknowingly gave me 25 years of autism experience, and encouraged, supported and loved me through the highs and lows.

ACKNOWLEDGEMENTS

Thanks to my parents who encouraged me to be independent and pursue my dreams and goals.

Thanks to the young people who I have had the pleasure to teach over the past twenty two years and in particular those with autism who have taught me far more than they will ever realise.

Thanks to the NAKMAS National Governing Body for their support and backing on this and other education and autism related projects over the past twenty years.

Thanks to my friend and colleague Dr Luke Beardon, Senior Lecturer in Autism at Sheffield Hallam University without whom my writing would not be where it is now, and whose support and encouragement enabled me to achieve my precious Doctorate in Education.

Thanks to NAKMAS Publishing for believing in me and my work.

And finally, thanks to my students Nel, Erin, Oliver and Alfie who agreed to help with the photographs for the book, as well as photographer Sam Austin of Sam Austin Design, who was also a student as a child.

5

FOREWORD

'I was only six years old when introduced to Martial Arts, and it was this age I was diagnosed with Asperger's syndrome. At this point to say I was an unconventional 'oddball' would be an understatement. My social skills were poor, I didn't mix well at school but most importantly I was a dreamer with no sense of discipline or direction. Little did I know this would be the point where all that was going to change.

When Sandra became my Sensei she didn't see me in this way at all. She made me realise my potential, not just in Karate but how I could develop as a human being. After six years I developed into a confident and committed student, going on to teach others in the class at just the age of nine. I went as far as 2nd Kyu (brown one stripe) before I had to prioritise my education, but I will most certainly be back to finish what I started'.

Tom, aged 22

'I have Asperger's Syndrome. I like karate classes, because they provide you with self-defence skills that can help you all through life. Also in the classes you can form far-reaching friendships with many people; teachers and fellow students alike'.

Alfie, aged 13

'Being autistic is not always easy. I find it hard to make friends because they are not interested in the same things. Joining a kung fu club was the best think I have done. Everyone is friendly, I get to learn new things and it helps me with my confidence, co-ordination and balance. I recommend it to everyone I know'.

Abigail, aged 12

CONTENTS

Foreword

Introduction   8

1. About You   11

2. What Are Martial Arts?   12

    Why Are They Good For Me?   13

    What Should I Choose?   14

3. Preparing For A Class   16

    What To Wear?   17

    What Next?   19

4. During A Class   21

    Martial Arts Techniques   24

    Language   32

    Buddies   33

    Dos and Don'ts   34

    Sensory Issues & Overload   35

5. Related Activities   41

6. Teacher Tips   45

7. Helpful Information & Contacts   50

INTRODUCTION

Thank you so much for choosing to open this book. Let me tell you a bit about myself, and why and how I have written it.

I consider myself an educator first and foremost. I have a Doctorate in Education with a professional research interest in autism within educational situations. I have a personal research interest in sensory issues surrounding autism. I am a 6th Dan black belt in karate and have practised in tai chi and yoga.

For over twenty years I have taught martial arts and dance. A chance encounter with an autistic student some fifteen years ago set me off on an autism discovery; both as part of my teaching, and personally.

I had a late adult clinical diagnosis of Asperger's Syndrome and have since been an enthusiastic advocate, promoting awareness and acceptance in my writing and as a speaker at conferences and training events.

My website 'the autistic voice' (details found on page 50) takes forward the ethos of my doctoral thesis which was based methodologically on voices (perspectives) of the children and young people who took part in the research. I also write a blog and have a Facebook page, both of the same name.

You will have seen this continued theme in the Foreword, where I opened it up to my students to have their say, as they are the experts about their experiences and expectations.

The Book

This book has been written primarily for the young autistic person who has considered taking up a martial art, but has not known where to start or what to expect. It also gives guidance for parents,responsible adults and teachers. It includes detail of what may happen, what choices may need to be made, and suggestions for coping with any difficulties.

This is not a book about autism but the guidance is based on the signs and characteristics usually seen in an autistic individual.

It is not presumed that all autistic individuals are the same or will experience the same issues. In fact I am very much of the opinion that all students should be treated as individuals and as a martial arts teacher myself, I always ensure I get to know students to find out how I can best help them.

The content of the book is based on my experiences as a martial arts teacher, fifteen of which have been specialised in teaching children on the autism spectrum and with other related conditions. It is also based on extensive research on the learning experiences of young autistic individuals as part of my doctoral thesis over a period of four years and myself as an autistic person of course.

I have written the book using 'autistic person' as this is my personal preference. I realise that others may prefer to use 'person with autism'. I do not wish to offend anyone by my personal choices. I also use the term 'teacher' rather than 'coach' or 'instructor' as I see the role as an educator.

STUDENT TIPS

These tips are from autistic students who currently practise martial arts. They may apply to you or not, but they are simply something to think about.

PARENT ADVICE

This advice is designed to help you as a parent or responsible adult make informed decisions.

You have been told you are autistic, or to put it another way, have a diagnosed autism spectrum condition (ASC, sometimes called autism spectrum disorder, ASD).

This may mean different things to each of you. If you are on the autism spectrum you will have differences within three areas in some way:

1. Social Interaction – the way you relate to another person socially

2. Communication - exchanging information with another person

3. Behaviour – your words, actions and mannerisms

There will also be some sensory differences. This is often the area which stands out in a learning situation.

I expect you have one or more special interests... perhaps computer games, reading, dinosaurs, or looking after animals?

You may have seen films or television programmes with martial arts, or have school friends, siblings or neighbours who practise and have asked you to join them.

But you don't know what to expect or how good it will be for you. Will I like it? Will I be able to do it?

'I can help you find out more'

As well as being a martial arts teacher, I look after lots of different martial arts clubs and speak with teachers during my day job running a national martial arts governing body, and I am also diagnosed autistic, so I understand what might worry you.

If you would like to find out more about autism, there are lots of books and videos available. There are some links in the last section of the book.

2. WHAT ARE MARTIAL ARTS?

'Martial arts' is a term used to generally describe different training systems used for self-defence and lots of other good stuff.

There are some martial arts which most people have heard of… karate, kung fu; both seen in versions of the film Karate Kid or in the film Kung Fu Panda. You may have watched Judo or Taekwondo in the Olympics or other televised sporting events.

There are lots and lots of different martial arts. Many of them originated in countries within Asia: Japan, China, Korea, Thailand, and the Philippines. Others, perhaps less known, are from countries including Brazil and Russia.

Martial arts are mainly split into two types (there are many more than the ones listed).

Throwing arts: judo, ju jitsu, aikido, kendo, hapkido

Standing arts: karate, taekwondo, kung fu, choi kwang do, tang soo do, jeet kune do, kickboxing

Some martial arts are gentler and may appear dance-like: capoeira or tai chi for instance.

Which martial art you practise will depend on a few things: where you live, whether you are joining friends or a sibling, when classes are and how they fit into your other activities, and especially important, which one is most suitable for your needs.

Why Are They Good For Me?

Practising martial arts is a fun way to keep fit. They can help you in so many different ways.

To start with they can help you physically. You may be uncoordinated, have difficulties with balance, judging speed and distance or simply struggle with remembering left and right. You may be dyslexic (difficulty with reading and writing words and letters) or dyspraxic (difficulty with coordination). Martial arts may help with all these things. They can also develop your stamina and flexibility.

All of these may be helped by the set routines you will learn: kicking, punching, locks and holds, patterns. What you learn exactly will depend on the martial art you choose.

There is another benefit, especially to someone who is autistic. Classes are usually very structured; they begin with warm up exercises and follow a routine of techniques which are practised over and over until you know them really well. You do not have to be as good as, or better than someone else. You just have to try your best and enjoy the class.

Martial arts should help your confidence grow. This will help you in lots of areas of your life.

It is a sad fact that autistic children as well as many others can often be bullied for no reason than they are different. This should not be tolerated and adults in your life should try to prevent or at least deal with this, but it is true that bullies seem to choose people they consider to be vulnerable or weak in some way.

Martial arts can make your mind as well as your body stronger. This means you can be more confident and appear to others less vulnerable.

If you want to make new friends, attending martial arts classes can also be a way of doing so in a safe place where others have the same interest as you.

Of course if you would rather just stick to learning new skills and increasing your knowledge, that is fine as well.

What Should I Choose?

Choosing a martial art is very personal and you should do lots of research before deciding which one is best for you. You can visit local clubs, ask friends, look at websites, and even watch videos on the internet to see what might suit you.

If you would like to practise lots of partner work, for example, you might like to try judo or ju jitsu. Remember you will be thrown by classmates and land on the floor a lot. If you prefer to stand and work alone more, you might be better suited to a standing art.

Consider what makes you uncomfortable or more comfortable. For example, do you prefer others not to touch you? Are you happy to work with a partner closely during the class? Would you like to learn a new language?

You might want to sit down with your parents or responsible adults and have a chat about how any autism concerns may affect what you choose.

"you might need to try out several clubs and teachers before finding the right one for you"

The most important thing is that you find a club which makes you feel comfortable. You might need to try out several clubs and teachers before finding the right one for you. That is okay. Teachers are used to new students trying classes, and they encourage you to do so.

Call the club instructor before you take your child to the class. Explain the way your child reacts to new activities, issues to look out for and possible ways of dealing with these. Ask the teacher about any previous experience with autism. While this is certainly useful and preferred, you also need to be satisfied that he or she does not have preconceived ideas of what your child may be like or need. A good teacher is one who is willing to be flexible and will get to know your child as an individual.

Also check that the instructor has public liability and professional indemnity insurance in place, and that students' insurance is available. The club should be a member of an appropriate national governing body which will provide useful guidance and regulations to the club, for example, child protection, health and safety, ethical guidance and access to disclosure checks.

A great thing about those of us who are autistic is that when we take up a new hobby, we like to find out all about it and I expect you probably love to do research. If not, I am sure your parents or other responsible adults, perhaps your school teacher will help you.

3. Preparing for a Class

Where to Go?

Martial arts classes are held in a variety of different venues.

Often they are held in leisure and sports centres; in the main sports hall, or sometimes in studios designed especially for fitness or dance classes. These studios may have big mirrors on some of the walls. This may seem a little intimidating but they can be useful for watching others secretly or correcting your own practice.

Classes can often be held in local schools. This may be your own school or another. Sports halls and gyms are common places within schools to hold classes. Sometimes they are run by the school and are called an after-school club, and sometimes by teachers who do not normally teach at the school.

Other venues for classes may be village halls, community or church halls. These are usually smaller and quieter venues.

It is important to find the right teacher first, rather than pick a preferred venue and hope that the teacher will be right for you.

Classes may often be advertised in local newspapers or bulletins, at libraries or town halls, at the venues themselves or on the internet or social media sites such as Facebook or Twitter. Asking friends or family for recommendations is also a very good way of finding a suitable class.

It is a good idea to visit the venue before the day you start your class to see what to expect. Perhaps watch a class or two, or just get the feeling of the venue, where the toilets and changing rooms are, how bright it is, and so on. You might be able to make adjustments to help you cope with the environment or at least get used to it.

So, you have found a class to try. Fantastic. How exciting!

What to Wear

The first thing to know is what to wear. It is usual at the first few classes for a new student not to wear the class uniform. Generally it is best to wear loose tracksuit bottoms and a t-shirt.

Most martial arts are practised with bare feet (so make sure they are clean). Some including kung fu and taekwondo, sometimes wear special shoes, but do not worry about these until the teacher tells you to get some.

If you have hair below your collar, or a very long fringe, you will need to make sure it is secured away from your face. It is very dangerous to practise a martial art if you cannot see clearly.

You must make sure your fingernails and toenails are short, so as not to hurt someone else by accident. You will also be asked to remove any jewellery and your watch or friendship bands. If you like to wear a particular item as a comfort or to help you in some way (for example remember your left from right), it may be allowed provided it is not likely to cause an injury to yourself or another student.

You will need to ask the teacher and explain why you would like to do this.

After a few lessons, if you are happy with the club, you will be asked to wear a special uniform. This will be different for each martial art and will usually be a jacket and trousers of some kind with a special belt or sash.

Some martial arts are practised in a t-shirt and trousers or shorts. Usually you can buy this uniform from the club. Often it will include special club badges or the name of the club on it.

The uniforms are hardwearing so you may find some fabrics used can be a bit rough or scratchy. If you find this is a problem for you because your skin is particularly sensitive, chat to the teacher who should be able to suggest a way to make it easier for you to wear.

One way is to wear a soft t-shirt underneath. You might also want to have someone cut out the labels inside to avoid unnecessary discomfort.

Whether you are wearing beginner clothes or a uniform, what you wear must be clean and ironed. It is important to look neat and tidy as this shows respect to the teachers and other students. It also sets a good example to other new students as you become more experienced.

STUDENT TIP

'I was so excited to receive my first uniform with the badges and belt. I couldn't wait to try it on. It was a bit rough at first, but mum washed it in fabric softener and it was okay after that. I was proud to wear it to my club each week.'

What Next?

It is always important to take an adult with you to a new class; mum, dad, aunt, grandpa or someone else who may be responsible for you. They should be there to make sure you are happy and comfortable with the teacher, the surroundings, and they can do the boring stuff – filling in forms, and checking that the teacher knows what to expect when you join the class.

It is worth chatting to the teacher at the start to let him or her know what your likes and dislikes are, what makes you feel comfortable or uncomfortable, how to help you if they notice you are not coping well, what you want from the class. If you are a bit scared to do this, ask the adult with you to do it instead.

It is important to tell the teacher if you are happy to let other students know about your autism if necessary.

Some classes will have lots of students with autism and other conditions; for example, dyslexia or ADHD, and many of the students in these classes will be more understanding than some people you may have met in other places.

It is always your choice though and the teacher will respect this.

You should be asked to complete a form which will screen for health and related issues. It will also likely ask for details such as address, date of birth, contact telephone number and general practitioner details. These are required by the clubs legally for new young students and are useful for any emergency situations prior to, during or following a class. It is important that you give the club, telephone numbers which can definitely be reached during a class.

You should be given some kind of literature at the initial class to tell you about the club, what is expected from the students and what you should expect from the club.

It is recommended that you watch at least the whole of the first class as you have no idea how your child will react and if there is a problem, the teacher can consult you. After that you can be guided by the club teacher.

It is _essential_ that you tell the teacher if you or your child _does not_ want him or her to refer to the autism during the class. Many experienced teachers in this field are very open about such issues often encouraging the children to look out for each other's differences, in order to support, and to promote positive awareness of differences. Of course they will be happy to follow your lead if you tell them otherwise.

You must always bring your child into the class and collect him or her from the class rather than drop and collect from the car park. The teacher must know that the child is safe and especially so for a potentially vulnerable child. In addition, if there are issues which need to be discussed, for example in relation to learning or teaching, they can be dealt with as they arise rather than several weeks later or via the telephone or email.

4. During a Class

Initially

You will probably be asked to line up to begin the class. If you are new, someone will tell you where to line up. Often the line of students will be standing in grade order with the highest grade students at one end, and the beginners at the other end. Some martial arts prefer rows or columns instead. Some clubs will ask you to kneel down on the floor so that you can practise a formal bow. You may be asked to close your eyes while you do this. When this formal beginning is over, you will then need to do warm up exercises. You may do these as a whole class, or be put into smaller groups.

Bow

All martial arts have some kind of formal standing or kneeling bow. This is a sign of respect to the training hall, the martial art, the teachers and the other students. In karate this is practised with the feet together and the hands by the side of the body. In kung fu, it is practised with the feet together and the hands in the front of the body – one hand in a 'praying' position and the other fist in the hand. There will be other ways of bowing for your chosen martial art but your teacher will show you how and explain when and why this is necessary.

Warm up

All physical classes should always begin with warm up exercises. These exercises will help to gently stretch your muscles and joints to get them ready for performing the martial art techniques, so that you do not hurt yourself. The exercises are also designed to help your heart and lungs cope with the physical movements, most of which will need lots of energy and effort to perform well. There are some exercises which will help you with any balancing difficulties and as your body becomes stronger you should find your balance improves.

Some examples of warm up exercises are shown here:

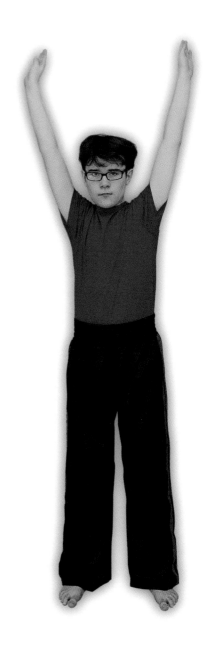

BALANCE EXERCISE

ARMS CIRCLING

FLOOR EXERCISE FOR STRETCHING LEGS

FORWARD STANCE STRETCH

If you feel unwell or are injured at any stage of your class it is important to tell the teacher immediately.

Try not to hold your breath as you exercise or practise martial arts. It is dangerous and will be very uncomfortable. Your teacher may show you special ways of breathing during your practice. This will help your stamina and may be useful in times of anxiety or stress.

If you feel any pain, stop and tell the teacher.

Martial Arts Techniques

What kinds of techniques you learn will depend on what martial art you have chosen. However, there are many common techniques performed in different martial arts and I am going to give you some examples.

Stances

A stance is simply a way to stand. There are many stances in martial arts and they are all designed to make the techniques easy and effective to perform. They have different names in different martial arts but I will use the basic words to describe them. In kung fu for instance, stances are usually named after animals or birds, for example, crane stance.

The most basic stance is simply the **standing stance** which is used at the start of the class and during the class in between techniques and other more complex stances. It can be used simply when you are standing to listen to the teacher or 'relaxing' during the class. You may have your feet parallel and shoulder width apart with your arms in front slightly (see page 18) or in this photo the kung fu position is different. The exact positioning will depend on the martial art.

Another stance used in many martial arts is a **front or forward stance**. This involves one leg being forward and the other back, both feet pointing towards the front. The front knee is usually bent and the back knee straight. In some martial arts this stance is very low, in others much higher.

As you are practising a combat system in martial arts, an important stance is the **fighting stance**. This may differ slightly in different martial arts, but generally one foot is forward of the other, with both knees bent. Your weight is in the middle so that it is a very strong stance. From this stance, you can spar (or fight) or practise techniques, kicks for example, in a more relaxed manner to other more formal stances.

There is another stance which is commonly used, and this is the **horse stance** (sometimes called **horse-riding stance**, or in judo, **defensive stance**). Usually the legs are wide apart, with the feet facing the front and the knees quite bent, although this will change slightly according to the martial art. It is a strong stance.

The last main stance is the **back stance**, and this one especially can be very different depending on the martial art. It basically has more weight on the back leg than the front leg but the position of the legs and feet will be taught by your teacher to make sure they are right for your own practice.

There will be additional stances depending on the martial art you choose.

Punches

Several martial arts incorporate punches, for example, karate, taekwondo, kickboxing, choi kwang do, kung fu and others. Punches are useful as the fist is a 'weapon' you have with you all the time. The punches will all be similar but there may be differences which you will learn from your own teacher. There are many types of punch with changes in direction, height, speed and power.

It is very important that you hold your fist in a way which is safe to punch with. Normally you will clench your fist tightly, placing the thumb on the outside. When you practise a basic punch, you point the two biggest knuckles towards your target; these are stronger and will be more effective. Punching with the smaller knuckles may cause injury.

Kicks

There are many types of kicks practised in martial arts. Some are direct kicks. For example, **front kick** which is aimed at the target's stomach or higher. Other kicks are indirect, for example a **roundhouse kick**. For these types of kicks, you rotate your hips to give more power. Kicks can be low, medium or high. Some involve jumping or spinning.

Blocks

Blocks are moves using the arms designed to stop attacks from punches, kicks and strikes. They are usually practised fast and the arms need to be quite relaxed so that they can move quickly. Some martial arts use stronger arms for blocking. Blocks can also be practised using the legs.

Strikes

Strikes vary a lot in different martial arts. In karate for instance, they are similar to punches, using different parts of the hand, or used with elbows, forearm or wrists. In ju jitsu a strike is more of a distraction technique. Strikes are considered important in kung fu and can involve the knees, feet, back and hips as well.

Throws

In martial arts which specialise more in 'throwing' you will be taught lots of safety techniques before you are taught the actual throws. You will be taught to **break your fall**, so that you fall safely and can protect yourself and get back up quickly. You will usually be taught to **slap** the floor as you fall, which will remove some of the force of landing. You will also be taught to do rolls, for example, a **forward roll** which can be used to escape an opponent.

All martial arts which teach throws and falls are practised on special mats which cushion the floor and make it safer and more comfortable for you.

To practise a good throw, you need to use the strength of your hips and legs and good timing. You must never practise these without supervision until you know what you are doing and your teacher is happy for you to do so.

Sweeps

Sweeps are used to knock your opponent off his or her feet. You can use your legs, feet or hands.

Patterns

Patterns are a series of moves ranging from easy to more complex. The moves are designed to flow together so they are considered quite 'dance-like' in some martial arts. In karate these patterns are called kata and in taekwondo they are poomse. If you watch a class performing patterns, it is like watching army soldiers. Everyone moves together and practises time and time again.

If the movements were used separately they could be very useful as defensive movements for street self-defence. Many classes teach students how to use the movements in this way.

Sparring or Fighting

The thought of fighting in class might seem a bit scary at first, but as a beginner you will not be expected to get it right all the time. You will usually be asked to partner someone who has lots of experience and this person can help you as you go along, giving you examples of what you can do. An experienced partner will also be better at controlling his or her movements to ensure you do not get hurt in any way.

If your teacher sees anything which could be dangerous, the fight will be stopped immediately. It is also an opportunity to watch what others do and perhaps copy just one move so that you gradually get better.

You will often have to wear some protective pads on your hands and legs for this part of your practice. These are only to protect you and not an excuse for your opponent to strike you harder. The type of protective pads worn will depend on the martial art. Some martial arts use head guards as well. If your club uses these and you have an issue with your face being covered, you will need to speak to the teacher to find a way to make it more comfortable for you.

Language

By practising a martial art there may be an opportunity to learn a new language. It will not be like languages at school, where you learn verbs and nouns, and how to buy a loaf of bread or post a letter.

The language you learn will be related to the martial art you are practising. In karate, judo, and aikido for instance you will learn some Japanese words. In kung fu they will be Chinese and in taekwondo, tang soo do, and choi kwang do, they will be Korean. Some martial arts and some teachers do not use the traditional language and therefore you will continue to describe the techniques in your usual language.

Ichi. Ni. San

However if you do have to learn a new language, do not be afraid of this. Most students enjoy learning the new words. Some teachers make up rhymes or find fun ways to help you learn and remember. You may be given word sheets to learn from at home, or sometimes be given little quizzes in class. When I teach I try to make learning the words into games.

STUDENT TIP

'If you struggle to learn the language, you can ask your teacher to help you record it. Then you can playback whenever you want to.

Also I make up rhymes to remember some of the words. It really helps me.'

You are likely to learn 'normal' words in the language as well: hello, goodbye, thank you, teacher, stop, go, right, left and numbers.

If you are ever unsure of what the teacher is saying or why, it is important to ask and not just to get anxious, upset or leave the room.

If you have difficulties learning words, do not worry about this. Just make sure your teacher knows. He or she can find ways to help you either to learn the words, or to make sure you know what techniques to do in class. One method I use is to ask students what a particular word means, and this often helps other students who are unsure.

Another way is for the teacher or someone else to record the words for you, so that you can listen and learn in your own time.

Buddies

It can be useful for new and beginner students to be given a **buddy** in the class. This is simply someone with more experience who can help you with any questions, show you where to stand, where to find things, and generally just be there in case of need or difficulty. The buddy does not replace the teacher but is an additional person who can be trusted. The buddy is also useful if there is a change of teacher one week, or for a rare change in hall for some reason. The buddy is a 'comfort' for the autistic student. The teacher may even allocate two buddies, in case one is absent for sickness or holidays.

> **STUDENT TIP**
>
> 'I was appointed as a buddy for a younger student of a lower grade. I have loved having the extra responsibility and when my buddy passed his grading recently, I felt really proud, of him and myself.
>
> Ask for a buddy in your class. You will find it really helpful.'

Personally I select buddies based not only on experience, but also on the needs of the buddy. For example, I may have an experienced child who is not so confident personally, who may benefit or thrive from taking some responsibility. In this way, buddies help and learn from each other. It is very important that buddies feel comfortable with each other, and continue to enjoy the experience, so it may be that they need to be changed from time to time. Students should be fully prepared for any such changes.

Dos and Don'ts

There are lots of rules in martial arts classes, usually called etiquette. Some are to ensure the students are safe, some are about respect of the martial art, the teachers and the students. They are all important. Lots of them are the same for all clubs, but there will probably be additional ones in your club which are necessary for you to know. I have listed some of the common dos and don'ts so that you are prepared.

DO

- Listen carefully to your teachers
- Be respectful to other students
- Shake hands at the end of working with a partner
- Bow when entering the training hall
- Put up your hand when you have a question or want to leave the room
- Spend time before the class practising or warming up your body
- Let your teacher know if you will be absent from a class
- Attend classes regularly
- Tell your teacher if you feel unwell or have an injury
- Tell your teacher if you are having a difficult day and need additional help or consideration
- Tell your teacher or parent if you are being bullied in any way, either in the club or outside, for example, at school

DON'T

- Eat in the training hall, unless given permission by your teacher
- Chew gum in the class
- Misbehave in the training hall or disrupt other students' learning
- Practise martial arts at school or with friends outside the class
- Forget your correct clothes including your belt if you wear one
- Be afraid to ask questions if you don't understand
- Compare yourself with other students and how they learn

Sensory Issues & Overload

Most autistic individuals experience sensory differences of some kind. They are not necessarily unpleasant but some may affect how you learn, and it will be useful for the teacher to know about these.

You are likely to be either hypersensitive (more sensitive) or hyposensitive (less sensitive) to certain things: sounds, light, heat and so on, than non-autistic individuals. This may cause you to feel uncomfortable sometimes. It can be difficult to explain these feelings to someone else who does not have them. If there are lots of things going on at once which make you feel uncomfortable, you can become 'overloaded' and this can often make you feel like you are going to 'explode'. Some autistic individuals get angry when they are 'overloaded' and others get anxious or panic and need to get away to a quiet place.

When you begin to train in a martial arts club you and your parents or responsible adults, need to explain to your teacher what might happen if you feel 'overloaded'. They should be prepared in advance so that they know what to do to help you.

It is useful for you to have a sign to show your teacher without having to speak, that you need quiet time; perhaps to leave the room for five or ten minutes to calm down. Perhaps you could form a letter T (= time out) with your hands, or have some other type of signal that your teacher understands immediately.

I have listed some possible sensory issues below with some suggestions for coping during your class:

Eye Contact

It is often difficult for autistic individuals to make eye contact. Even if you have this skill, you may find it quite uncomfortable. Students of martial arts are usually taught to look their opponent or partner in the eyes. If you find this difficult, a tip is to look between their eyebrows or even at their nose.

Fabric (uniform)

As I indicated earlier, your uniform fabric may be a bit rough or scratchy. This can be helped by wearing a soft t-shirt underneath and removing the labels.

Light

You will find often in large halls that the lighting is quite bright. These types of venues tend to use fluorescent lights. It is common for many autistic individuals to wear glasses with tinted glass to help block out some of this extreme brightness.

Noise (general)

Sports halls can become very noisy places: teachers calling instructions, students chattering, possibly spectators chattering, other activities next door, announcements over a loud speaker, and so on.

It can be difficult to change this, but there are ways your teacher can help to reduce the noise to some extent.

For instance, the centre staff could be asked to turn off the loudspeaker in the training hall and simply to come in to let the teacher know if there is an important announcement which affects the class.

Spectators could be asked to be quiet and take any babies or young children out if they start to make too much noise.

Martial arts are usually quite disciplined and students should not be talking during classes. You may find other students chatter too much at times, however, and if it becomes annoying have a quiet word with the teacher. As an autistic person you will be used to others trying to allow for your differences. There are some children who have ADHD or even autism for example, who find it difficult to keep quiet all the time. You also need to try to allow for their differences.

> **STUDENT TIP**
>
> 'Sometimes it gets a bit noisy in the class and it is difficult to concentrate. I find that if I try to focus on something in the room, even a mark on the wall, it helps me to forget what is around me. When I go to a course which I know might be noisy, I sometimes take little ear plugs – I can still hear the teacher but it drowns out background noise.'

Noise (sudden)

Some autistic individuals do not find noise a problem, but find sudden noise more uncomfortable.

One example of this may be a fire alarm sounding. As you will be training in a public place, this is a possibility. Your teacher will ask everyone to leave the building and stand in a certain place while staff and fire officers check that the building is safe for you to return to.

It is not something you should worry about as it rarely happens, but make sure your teacher knows how you are likely to react with sudden noise such as this, so that you can be helped and supported.

Smells

If you are hypersensitive to smells and aromas, you might want to be pre-warned. Sports halls can be pretty smelly places as many of the sports practised in them can involve lots of running around and clothes which are not all natural. Of course not all halls are smelly, but to you they may seem more so than to other non-autistic individuals. This might also apply to the changing rooms. This can easily be resolved by changing before you come to the venue, and wearing a jacket over the top to hide your uniform.

If there is a particular smell which you are hypersensitive to, for example, your teacher's perfume or aftershave, it is worth mentioning. I am sure your teacher would rather not wear it during classes, than allow it to make your learning experience uncomfortable.

Space (spatial awareness)

Some autistic individuals find it hard to judge distance so sometimes get very close to others without realising. It is useful here to put up your arms and stand an arm's distance away from the person next to you to give you both enough space.

It is also uncomfortable for some autistic individuals to have someone else standing too close. You can use the same solution here, or simply ask the other person to move a little further back. Your teacher can help here if this is a difficulty for you.

Use of Equipment

It may seem strange that this is listed under sensory issues.

For sparring (fighting) you will usually have to wear some kind of pads on your hands, legs and top of your feet. These may be stretchy pull on ones or chunkier ones made of PVC. What kind you use will depend on which martial art you practise. If one particular type is too uncomfortable, perhaps speak to your teacher who may be able to suggest an alternative for you. If you have any allergies to PVC or latex it is important to let the teacher know so that he or she can check the materials of any equipment, protective or otherwise.

Martial arts classes also use special kick and punch pads to practise on. If you have particular sensitivities it is important that your teacher is told.

Whistles

Sometimes during classes, whistles and bells are used as a means to attract students' attention, especially if it is a large hall or there are lots of students. For some autistic individuals this is a useful way to focus attention, and for others it can be quite uncomfortable. Talk to your teacher if you find this difficult to see if any alternatives can be used instead.

I once taught a very young student who had a poor attention span and his mum came to classes with a whistle to blow whenever he wandered out of the line. As an autistic teacher, I found it difficult to listen to a whistle every five minutes or so. We teachers sometimes find things difficult as well!

5. RELATED ACTIVITIES

Courses

These are likely to be similar to normal classes, but may be at a different time, day or in a different venue. If your club has several different classes, there may be students from other classes, which means there will be students you do not know from your normal class. There may also be additional teachers, or perhaps a guest teacher. This may be from inside your club or it may be someone who has been invited by your teacher, to take the course. This is usually an expert in a particular aspect of martial arts, or a teacher who is a high grade.

You may want to get to the course early so that you can become familiar with the hall, and any other things which may be different. Your teacher should make any new teachers aware of your learning needs. Other students who do not know you are unlikely to be able to accommodate your needs as well as your normal class mates so be aware of this and try not to let it upset you.

Grading Sessions

Grading sessions are what martial arts clubs call examinations. They are usually an opportunity for you to go to the next grade level or belt/sash colour. Some martial arts do not grade students and some simply use the terms beginner, intermediate and advanced.

How grading sessions are organised will depend on the martial art you choose and the club you attend.

Some grading sessions will take place during a normal class, or at your usual class time and venue. Others will be separately organised events, in the same way I described courses. They may be at a different venue and there may be a guest examiner.

If you are told you will be grading, it is a good idea to sit down with your teacher and ask for him or her to explain to you what will happen at the grading session.

Often when you pass your next level of grading, you will receive a certificate and depending on the martial art, a new coloured belt or sash. Some clubs give out additional smaller grades in between belts which are called tags. These are stitched to your belt or sash, or sometimes are little badges which are stitched to your suit.

Your own teacher will explain the result system to you as they differ a lot between clubs.

Whatever the martial art, there will be techniques set for each grade or level which you will need to perform to a good standard. Sometimes there will also be exercises set and questions asked.

Try not to worry about these grading sessions. They may seem a little scary but even your teacher and the examiner has gone through them as beginners and they really want you to do well.

Competitions

Not all clubs send students to competitions. If you are interested in these, it is worth telling your teacher when you begin. If the club does not take part in competitions, they can usually recommend another club to you.

Some clubs have competitions among their own students and these can be a good way to practise and get used to competing.

There are two types of competition: sparring (or fighting) and patterns.

Sparring competitions are between two individuals fighting for short periods of time. The winner of each fight then goes on to fight other winners.

Eventually there are just two remaining fighters who compete for first place and usually a trophy. They are overseen by two referees who are experienced teachers or examiners. Their job is to score points for winning techniques and decide at the end of the fight who has won. They also watch to make sure the fight is safe and can stop it if someone gets hurt.

Pattern competitions are where individuals compete against each other. You do not need a partner although sometimes there are team competitions where several people do the pattern at the same time and compete against other groups of people.

Judges score the way you perform the pattern. They look for good techniques, timing, presentation, and the points they score are added up to see who the winner is.

Again the winner will usually receive a trophy.

Competitions may be local to the club or may be a long distance away. They will often be in unfamiliar venues and it may take a while for you to feel comfortable. It might be worth getting to the venue as early as possible to make the transition easier for you.

Usually the teacher will go with students to a competition to support them and explain anything which may not be expected or the way things are done during a normal class. There will be lots of people watching the competition so usually your parents, guardians, family and friends will be able to go as well to support you.

It should always be your choice whether you enter a competition or not. Never feel pressured to do so. If you feel uncomfortable, let someone you trust know immediately.

Teaching (Coaching)

> **STUDENT TIP**
>
> 'I have attended a junior coaching course and I absolutely love to teach other students. It helps my confidence, and also helps other people which I love to do. I enjoy using my knowledge and skills and I give really good explanations because I remember all the details.'

As you get more experienced at your martial art, there may be an opportunity for you to help your teacher by teaching other students. This will help you build your confidence and leadership skills which will be useful in the training hall and outside at other activities. Some clubs will give their junior students special training to do this teaching.

If you are asked to do this, you should feel very special. It is an honour to help others and it will show that your teacher trusts you and your martial arts skills.

Autistic individuals can be very good teachers. We pay attention to detail and are able to give good and detailed explanations. If our martial art is one of our special interests, we are likely to have a lot of knowledge and skill.

6. TEACHER TIPS

You are either reading this book because you would like to open your classes to young autistic students, or because you already teach them. Either way the information thus far will be of interest and of use to you.

The following tips will be useful in addition to the information you have already read. If you are experienced in this field some tips you will know and others you may not, but as a teacher, I know that we should never stop educating ourselves. If like me you teach autistic students on a regular basis, you will know that you can learn as much from your students as they can from you. If you are new to this, you are very lucky as your autism journey is just beginning.

These tips come in equal measures from my own experiences and from young autistic students who are keen to pass on insider knowledge to help others.

The relationship between teacher and student should be one of trust and respect. Each will get to know the other more over weeks, months and even years. For the autistic student, if this trust and respect is broken it will be very difficult to mend. This relationship is paramount to the learning experience.

As I indicated earlier in this book, the ability to recognise each student as an individual with their own needs is crucial. You need to spend time to get to know your students; their likes, dislikes, what makes them uncomfortable, how you can help them achieve their goals... This can often be done during classes while engaging in question and answer sessions for example, or by watching them work with each other during group tasks.

As with all junior students and particularly with those more vulnerable, this of course must not be done outside of the class environment unless parents are present.

My research with young autistic individuals in informal learning situations including martial arts classes (Ellis, 2014) revealed many issues which affect their learning and these should be considered during your classes.

While these tips are primarily about your autistic students, many of them are also relevant for non-autistic young students as well. As I have mentioned, each student is an individual and not all tips apply to all students. These are also relevant for any autistic adult students.

a.   Students tend to enjoy constructive and detailed teaching with structure to the classes.

b.   Many students like to impress – to prove their worth or try to fit in. They may come across as extraverts or confident but you must realise that actually this may not always be true, and internally, they may feel very vulnerable and perhaps uncomfortable.

c.   Students like recognition and praise for a job well done. For autistic individuals this is even more so; they are often lacking in confidence and can have low self-esteem. Encouragement can be crucial to their learning experience.

d.   Students have high expectations and exacting standards, of themselves and their classes. This can lead to frustration, anxiety and rage.

e. Students have a tendency to copy or mimic behaviour. In young students especially, this tendency may result in unwanted or inappropriate behaviour simply because others exhibit these behaviours. Standing an autistic child next to such a child may either result in mimicking, or cause frustration or rage as the autistic child finds it an intolerable distraction.

f. Do not assume that autistic students will get on better with other autistic students. Like all children they either get on with each other or they do not! Often you will find they do not have patience for each other's differences, although sometimes they will complement each other.

g. Students usually have a literal understanding of language; therefore accurate and careful instructions are necessary, with the addition of reasons for and behind them. If the student understands, he or she is more likely to remember. Some autistic students can use the meanings to create pictures or visions, to aid memory.

h. You will need to allow more time for the students to learn new skills and activities. Often they will need to repeat them again and again before the memory is made. Once the memory is formed, however, you will likely find the student will never forget so make sure you do not make mistakes too often; you will never be allowed to forget them (as I know all too well from personal experience)!

i. Students also need time to process instructions before they are interrupted or given more instructions. This is especially important if they have to read text on paper or a whiteboard or similar before carrying out a task. My own autistic frustration is being expected to come up with a detailed answer while others are still talking. I have been known to leave the room just to 'think' on my own.

j. As I wrote earlier the relationship between student and teacher is paramount to the learning experience. Students can have a tendency to become over reliant on a teacher. Using named peer support or peer 'buddies' in the class is useful to prevent this as much as possible.

k. Students like the familiar – they expect and thrive on reliability, punctuality and consistency. If you say you are going to do something, they will expect you to do it. Being 'let down' in their eyes can affect them dramatically.

l. If there is more than one teacher in the class or group of classes, be aware that differing and conflicting instructions will confuse and irritate the students. This may lead to frustration, anxiety or anger.

m. You need to be aware of sensory overload in students – something which may seem minor to you may in fact affect the student in a major way. For example, an itchy label on clothing may seem insignificant but may ruin an hour's learning experience for the student. I have cut out many labels over the years of teaching.

n.   Students can become easily distracted; as a teacher, enthusiasm for the subject is key to keeping the student focused. Younger students enjoy a sense of humour in a teacher. As autistic individuals tend to say whatever is in their mind, regardless of appropriateness, this is a useful characteristic to have.

o.   You may find students will be affected by external factors: tiredness, bad day at school or work, lack of usual routine, hunger and so on. Try not to add to the pressure by taking the class in a different direction to normal or for that student at least. I realise this is not always simple.

p.   You are the professional. If after a few weeks, you are sure the child is not coping or settling, do not be afraid to speak to the parent and be honest. Whether the student is autistic or not, not all individuals are suited to martial arts, or your particular class.

q.   You should never make assumptions based on autism theory.

To reiterate, remember at all times, the student is an individual and as such will have his or her own needs, differences and experiences. As a good teacher it is your role to nurture these and to provide a safe, beneficial and enjoyable learning experience.

Teaching autistic individuals is very rewarding... a little more knowledge certainly helps smooth the path to success.

'When you teach a person with autism, They teach YOU'

Extra Reading

Attwood, T. (2008). *The Complete Guide to Asperger's Syndrome.* London: Jessica Kingsley Publishers.

*Ellis, S. J. (2014). Perspectives of the Autistic 'Voice': An Ethnography Examining Informal Education Learning Experiences. Published thesis, Sheffield Hallam University. http://shura.shu.ac.uk/8317/

Frith, U. (2008). *Autism: A Very Short Introduction.* Oxford: Oxford University Press.

Jackson, J. (2004). *Multicoloured Mayhem: Parenting the Many Shades of Adolescents and Children with Autism, Asperger Syndrome and AD/HD.* London: Jessica Kingsley Publishers.

Jackson, L. (2002). *Freaks, Geeks and Asperger Syndrome: A User Guide to Adolescence.* London: Jessica Kingsley Publishers.

Jordan, R. Powell, S. (1995). *Understanding and Teaching Children with Autism.* Chichester: Wiley & Sons Ltd.

Sainsbury, C. (2000). *Martian in the Playground: Understanding the schoolchild with Asperger's Syndrome.* London. Paul Chapman Publishing.

Wing, L. (1996). *The Autism Spectrum.* London: Constable and Robinson Ltd.

Useful Websites

Martial Arts Illustrated (magazine) www.martialartsunltd.co.uk

*National Association of Karate and Martial Art Schools (NAKMAS National Governing Body) www.nakmas.org.uk

National Autistic Society (autism based resources/training) www.autism.org.uk

*The Autistic Voice (my own website with links to blog, Facebook page and Twitter) www.theautisticvoice.co.uk

* connected to my own work

**"It is both a privilege and a pleasure to teach a child with AUTISM.
My experiences have made me a better person."**

Dr Sandra Beale-Ellis

MY MARTIAL ARTS' ACTION PLAN

-
-
-
-
-
-
-
-
-
-
-
-
-
-
-
-